the opentable vol. 2
an invitation to **walk** with God

the **opentable** vol. 2
an invitation to **walk** with God

participant's guide

Jason **Clark**
Foreword by Donald **Miller**

THOMAS NELSON
Since 1798

NASHVILLE   DALLAS   MEXICO CITY   RIO DE JANEIRO

Published in Nashville, Tennessee, by Thomas Nelson. Thomas Nelson is a registered trademark of Thomas Nelson, Inc.

Published in association with Alive Communications.

Thomas Nelson, Inc., titles may be purchased in bulk for educational, business, fund-raising, or sales promotional use. For information, please e-mail SpecialMarkets@ThomasNelson.com.

Unless otherwise noted, Scripture quotations are taken from the HOLY BIBLE: NEW INTERNATIONAL VERSION®. © 1973, 1978, 1984 by International Bible Society. Used by permission of Zondervan Publishing House. All rights reserved.

Scripture quotations marked CEV are from THE CONTEMPORARY ENGLISH VERSION. © 1991 by the American Bible Society. Used by permission.

Scripture quotations marked ESV are from THE ENGLISH STANDARD VERSION. © 2001 by Crossway Bibles, a division of Good News Publishers.

Scripture quotations marked KJV are from THE KING JAMES VERSION.

Scripture quotations marked MSG are from *The Message* by Eugene H. Peterson. © 1993, 1994, 1995, 1996, 2000. Used by permission of NavPress Publishing Group. All rights reserved.

Scripture quotations marked NKJV are from THE NEW KING JAMES VERSION. © 1982 by Thomas Nelson, Inc. Used by permission. All rights reserved.

ISBN: 978-1-4185-1089-3

Printed in the United States of America
10 11 12 13 14 15 (WC) 6 5 4 3 2 1

Related Products

The Open Table DVD, Volume 1: An Invitation to Know God

The Open Table Participant's Guide, Volume 1: An Invitation to Know God

The Open Table DVD, Volume 2: An Invitation to Walk with God

Contents

Foreword by Donald Miller. 9

Acknowledgments 11

An Invitation to the Open Table. 13

WEEK 1: The Love of God 17

WEEK 2: How Do We Interact with God? 39

WEEK 3: Does God Care about
Community?. 59

WEEK 4: What Does Faith Look Like? 81

WEEK 5: On Earth as It Is in Heaven 105

Foreword

We often think of spirituality in mushy, sentimental terms. And if not mushy and sentimental, we think of spirituality like voodoo or magic, as though we are creating formulas to make magical things happen. I want to propose that spirituality is neither mushy nor magical. The same God toward whom we address our spiritual concerns is the same God who made food come from the ground. And food doesn't come from the ground through magical formulas. Crops are grown from seeds, and only if those seeds are planted in the right season, and only if those seeds are planted in good soil, and only if that soil gets a share of sunlight, and even then it all must be watered. In other words, spirituality takes work, just like everything in life, everything that God created.

This book is more a farm guide than a book of spells. If you want to know God, my friends have created a guide to cultivating and nurturing your soul in such a way that something can grow, something that will sustain you, namely, a relationship with God.

Like crops from the soil, relationships take work and time and intentionality. When you meet a Christian who is calm, patient, and forgiving, you are meeting somebody who has what the Bible calls the *fruit of the Spirit*. That phrase refers not to any sort of magic or wish fulfillment but to gifts given by God to a person who submitted to the conditional requirements needed for fruition in their character. These people don't walk around hearing God's voice in their heads, and they don't float through life like clouds. What the fruit does in their lives, again, is not magic or mush. Rather, these people experience emotional health and stability. This is the great benefit of spirituality, that we find ourselves centered and wise, unaffected by the emotional crescendos of earthly events.

This book is also designed to be used in community. You can't tend a farm on your own, and your soul is too complex to grow fruit without the help of others. Even God chooses to live in community.

As you and your friends go through this book, don't ask what principle you can learn that will give you some sort of magical fulfillment. Instead, ask yourself, and ask each other, where the work is that will make the fruit grow. If you do this, I promise that in the months and years to come, your soul will bear fruit.

Enjoy the work,
Donald Miller

Acknowledgments

I want to thank my brother Joel, my hero, for involving me in Volume Two of *The Open Table*. I am grateful to Don Miller and Thomas Nelson for believing in this project as well. I want to thank my entire family, especially Uncle Shelly, my wife, Karen, and my dad and mom as they greatly influenced the writing. This book has also been wonderfully influenced by some of my mentors, men I've yet to meet but whose writings and sermons have impacted my God journey. Thank you, Bill Johnson, Kris Valloton, and Dan Mohler. This book is dedicated to my wife, Karen, the most amazing person I will ever know, and my brilliant kids, Madeleine True, Ethan Wilde, and Eva Blaze—these are my favorite people in the whole world. I can't wait to see how God's love works through their lives! Above all, thank you, God, for your always-good love.

Jason Clark

An Invitation to the Open Table

First of all, this is not homework. This isn't some weekly school assignment that you will rush to complete and then be graded on. Think of it more as an independent study of your beliefs and thoughts.

Each week you will be asked to read five daily sections before meeting in your Open Table group. If you don't have a group, we encourage you to find others who are participating in the Open Table series or who might be interested in participating, because group discussion can be invaluable.

In order to get the most out of this experience, you need only to be honest with yourself and with your answers. You don't have to share all of your answers with the group if you don't want to, just as long as you put some honest thought into what the stories and questions mean for your life. Having said that, both you and your group will benefit the most when everyone agrees to participate fully.

Each week's study is broken into five days. And within each of the days, there are stories and closing thoughts. When you are reading the daily sections, try to concentrate on how the story or message can be applied to your life and don't be afraid to make notes or write out your answers.

At the end of the week, there will be several pages of small group discussion questions that cover the material you read for the week. You may answer those before you meet with your group or during the meeting. The important thing is that you participate and learn a little about yourself and about the other participants in your group in the process.

Now, you might be shy or you might be a fearless public speaker. Either way, your thoughts and opinions are important and you should feel free to share your answers without judgment.

Likewise, we ask that you keep an open mind and an open heart as the other group members share their answers and thoughts. It's called Open Table for a reason—everyone is welcome and everyone is equal.

Sounds pretty simple, doesn't it? Let's get started.

For you were once darkness, but now you are light in the Lord. Live as children of light (for the fruit of the light consists in all goodness, righteousness and truth).

—Ephesians 5:8–9

the
open**table** vol. 2
an invitation to **walk** with God

The Love
of God

Opening Thoughts

- When you see the phrase "God is love," what does that mean to you? Does it sound like something Christians are supposed to say, or do you truly understand the implications of those words in your life?

- Have you ever turned away from God because you thought something you have done or said was just too much to be forgiven?

- What do you think would happen if you realized that no matter how imperfect you are, God still loves you and pursues a relationship with you?

■ Day 1: The Butterfly Effect

Before the "butterfly effect" was a movie, it was a phrase coined to describe the scientific theory of a man named Edward Lorenz. This theory states that the seemingly small movement of a butterfly's wings on one side of the world can create a chain of events leading to powerful winds of change halfway around the planet.

This is how the love of God has moved in my life. Each time I think I understand his love, I encounter him in a new way, the butterfly moves its wings, and my world is profoundly and forever changed.

God is love. If you have met him, you already know this firsthand. If you haven't yet met him, you should consider introducing yourself. And just in case we forget, the Bible reminds us:

"Whoever does not love does not know God, because God is love" (1 John 4:8).

I like the analogy of the butterfly effect. It fits with how God has revealed himself to me. Because he is love, he comes as the butterfly, gentle and beautiful. But I've also learned that once I receive his love, I am introduced to the tornado of his life-altering love. His love consumes me and blows me off the course I had planned for myself so that I can better see the path he has planned for me. This love is my salvation, my rescue, and my provision. It's my strength, my hope, and my joy. God's love is an all-consuming phenomenon that encompasses every particle of me—if I let it.

Am I scaring you? Well, it is a little scary, but in a very good way.

Like the butterfly wings, God is always gently whispering to me, "I love you." I hear it when I am surrounded by my family or when my kids laugh. I hear it when I'm out for a run or when I'm reading a good book or when a song plays on my iPod.

In fact, I am fully convinced that God is always, and in every way, whispering one thing to us: "I love you." What I have also learned is that his message of love is always followed by a question: "Do you believe me?"

This journey with God is about one thing—believing he loves us. Everything else we will look at over the coming days is grounded in this one truth: God is completely and absolutely in love with us, and his greatest desire is that we believe it.

As we learn how to believe him in the gentle whisperings of the butterfly wings, we will begin to engage the power of the tornado. The love of God is engaged when we say yes, when we believe. The power of God's love is then displayed in his mercy, grace, hope, healing, joy, provision, strength, and goodness. God knows that when we truly believe he loves us, we have access to all his love promises.

Our belief and acceptance that he loves us starts a chain reaction in our lives. When we believe that God has only one thought about us—"I love you"—the butterfly moves its wings (Romans 8:38–39). When we believe that he removes our sins as far as the east is from the west, the butterfly moves its wings (Psalm 103:12). When we believe that our old sinful nature is dead and we are a new creation in Christ, the butterfly moves its wings (2 Corinthians 5:17). And when we believe that everything he has is ours, the butterfly moves its wings enough to create change in every area of our lives (Luke 15:11–32).

Our new identity as followers of Jesus is found in believing that he loves us and in believing that "neither death nor life, neither angels nor demons, neither the present nor the future, nor any powers, neither height nor depth, nor anything else in all creation, will be able to separate us from the love of God that is in Christ Jesus our Lord" (Romans 8:38–39). Every question life throws at us is answered through a greater revelation of God's love.

We have been invited into the greatest love story of all time. The Creator of the universe, who is love, has extended his heart of love to us. He has invited us to believe, engage his love, and *become* love with him. I'm convinced that this new life—the one we gave to Jesus—is about learning how to believe God when he tells us he loves us.

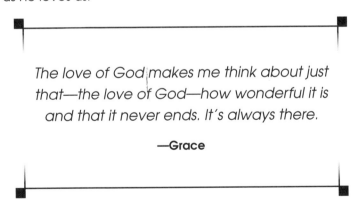

The love of God makes me think about just that—the love of God—how wonderful it is and that it never ends. It's always there.

—Grace

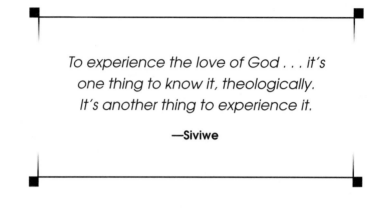

To experience the love of God . . . it's one thing to know it, theologically. It's another thing to experience it.

—Siviwe

Closing Thoughts

Do you really believe you are loved? How is God whispering his love to you today?

If you let the love of God flow through you, how do you show that love to other people? How are you showing God that you love him today?

■ Day 2: He Loves Me Best

Several years ago, while reading the gospel of John, I realized that John, the author, had a unique way of referencing himself. Three times he wrote about himself in the third person as the "one Jesus loved":

- "One of them, the disciple whom Jesus loved, was reclining next to him" (John 13:23).

- "So she came running to Simon Peter and the other disciple, the one Jesus loved" (John 20:2).

- "The disciple whom Jesus loved was following them" (John 21:20).

I grew up hearing preachers refer to John as Jesus' favorite, and how Jesus just had a special spot in his heart for John. As a kid I thought it was kind of cool that Jesus had a best friend. So when I discovered that John was the one who started the rumor, well, I was surprised. It was almost as if he was saying, "Oh, by the way, I don't know if you have heard this yet, but Jesus loves me best."

Still, the more I thought about it, the more I realized that if anyone knew about Jesus and his love, it was the disciples, and John was one of them. He was with Jesus for three years. He was there when Jesus was moved with compassion and healed two blind men (Matthew 20:29–34). He was there when Jesus wept before raising his friend Lazarus from the dead (John 11:38–43). He was there when Jesus healed, restored, delivered, forgave, and fed people. John ate, slept, prayed, laughed, cried, and did life with Jesus. He witnessed with his own two eyes the Love that is Jesus, poured out to the lost, weak, blind, and deaf. You name the need, John watched love meet it.

John then witnessed Love whipped, beaten, spit upon, and cursed. He watched as Jesus was nailed to and hung on a cross. John saw love in human form give up his life for all of mankind.

And then John was there for the resurrection, when Love displayed his nail-scarred hands and feet to the disciples. John watched Love ascend to heaven, and he experienced Love again when it descended in the form of the Holy Spirit. If anyone knew what love looked like, it was John.

This same disciple who wrote about himself as "the one Jesus loved" went on to write a book about love and all he had witnessed. In essence, the man who knew intimately what love looked like and felt like and acted like went on to tell us that Jesus—who *was* love—loved him best. You see, from John's perspective, Jesus was able to love him best without undermining his love for someone else. John's revelation is astounding: Jesus can love each of us as "the one." How cool is that?

The Bible says that when Jesus went to the cross, he did it "for the joy set before him" (Hebrews 12:2). You, me, and the guy sitting next to me at Starbucks—we are that joy. Jesus loves each of us individually and intimately. Because he went to the cross, we can know Jesus' love in such a way that, like John, we can say with absolute certainty: "I am the one Jesus loves best."

For me, it's been the tough times where I've more clearly felt God's love. It's the times I didn't deserve forgiveness and I got forgiveness. Or I didn't deserve grace and I got grace. There were times I felt forgotten by the world and God still held me tight and knew that I was there.

—Tim

Closing Thoughts

Do you agree with the idea that a unique relationship with Jesus is available to you? Why or why not? How could it affect your life if you choose to believe that you are the one Jesus loves; that he loves you best today?

If you believed that God loved you unconditionally, how would it change the way you interact with others? How would it change the way you felt about yourself?

■ Day 3: To Love in Turn

When I began thinking about how John referred to himself as "the one Jesus loved" and how this revelation of God's love is available to us, God began to speak to my heart. I started thinking about John's understanding of Jesus' love and wondered if I was capable of loving in the same way.

Recently, while at the supper table with my family, I told my wife she was the one I loved, that I loved her best, and that she was my favorite. I then looked at my oldest daughter and told her the same thing. I moved on to my son and then finally to my youngest daughter, repeating myself as I went: "You are the one I love . . ." And you know what? It was true and everyone at the table knew it. Somehow I am able to love each of them best.

Paul tells us in Romans 8:11 that the same Spirit who raised Christ from the dead lives in us. It stands to reason then that we should be able to love as Jesus does. In fact, I believe that is why we are here on earth. We exist to know God's love and to love him and others in turn. That is what this new life we have entered into is all about. The moment we surrender to God's love, the moment we receive our salvation, we say yes to love, and we say yes to *becoming* love to others.

The Christian journey isn't just about going to church; it's about becoming the church. It isn't just about going to heaven when we die; it's about bringing heaven to earth while we live. It isn't just about receiving the beautiful love of our Savior and friend Jesus; it's about becoming that same love—even to strangers. And I am convinced that the only way to become love is to know Jesus' love as John did.

Several years ago, I began dialoging with God from John's perspective. When praying, I would thank God for his love—not the broad and somewhat vague concept of love but the personal, intimate, one-of-a-kind love God has for me. I don't pray this way out of insecurity or arrogance. On the contrary, I have found that the more aware I am of how much God loves me, the greater capacity I have to love those around me. I can say to others, "You are the one I love."

A person can't give away what he or she doesn't possess. That's why it is so important that we begin to see ourselves as God does, thereby possessing love and giving it away in greater measure. I encourage you today to ask God to love you best, and then begin to love those around you.

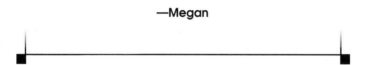

Receiving God's love and sitting in his presence and knowing that he accepts me and likes me and loves me the way I am is really profound and has changed the way I live my life.

—Megan

Closing Thoughts

Who in your life can you choose to "love best" today? What simple acts of kindness can you show to others?

There will be times when you don't feel very loved. What are some ways you can remind yourself that God loves you best? Are there certain songs, special places, or specific people who remind you of God's love?

■ Day 4: Religion and Relationship

In Exodus 19, Moses went up a mountain to meet with God and receive the Ten Commandments. Scripture says there was "thunder and lightning, with a thick cloud over the mountain, and a very loud trumpet blast. . . . Mount Sinai was covered with smoke because the LORD descended on it in fire. The smoke billowed up from it like smoke from a furnace, the whole mountain trembled violently, and the sound of the trumpet grew louder and louder" (vv. 16–19).

When Moses came down the mountain, the Israelites were afraid: "When the people saw the thunder and lightning and heard the trumpet and saw the mountain in smoke, they trembled with fear. They stayed at a distance and said to Moses, 'Speak to us yourself and we will listen. But do not have God speak to us or we will die'" (Exodus 20:18–19).

Upon seeing the glory of God, even from a distance, the Israelites forgot the love God revealed to them when he saved them from the slavery of Egypt. Instead of running to God, they basically said, "Hey Moses, we don't want a relationship with this God. He's too scary. Just tell us what his rules are and what he wants us to do." God heard them and gave them what they asked for—a set of beliefs involving devotional and ritual observances and a moral code governing the conduct of human affairs. In essence, religion without the relationship.

When we live outside of a loving relationship, life has to be determined by rules, but when we live within a relationship that is centered in love, life is no longer determined, maintained, or bound by a list of "don'ts." It's quite the opposite. When we learn to believe God's love, we begin to see the world through his eyes. That's because when we engage God's love, we can't help but become transformed by it. Suddenly, life is not about "don'ts," but about love.

The odd thing about humanity is that, like the Israelites of the Old Testament, we often seek to interact with God through a set of rules instead of through a relationship. We tend to choose religion over love. But Jesus lived and died to change that. He replaced religion with relationship. And when he did this, he turned everything on its ear and another piece of his plan was engaged.

When Jesus rose from the dead, he effectively ended Christianity as a religion. Because we live on the other side of the cross, we have access to an intimate relationship with love. This journey with God is not about joining a system or an institution or an organization or a denomination. Being a Christian is simply about having a relationship of love with Jesus.

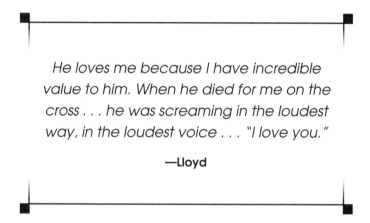

He loves me because I have incredible value to him. When he died for me on the cross . . . he was screaming in the loudest way, in the loudest voice . . . "I love you."

—Lloyd

Closing Thoughts

In what ways can you become less religious and more relational with God?

What are some circumstances you might find yourself in where you can extend the grace of God to others?

■ Day 5: Salvation, the Greatest Love Story

The story of Jesus' love is known as "the good news," or "the gospel." And in Romans 1:16, Paul wrote that this gospel is "the power of God for the salvation of everyone who believes." Because of Jesus, the distant God found through religion was suddenly a close God found through relationship. The love of God was and still is being experienced firsthand through salvation.

Today, we use the words *salvation* and *saved* so much in our vernacular that they have lost a little of their wonder. The New Testament uses the Greek word *sozo*, which means rescued, delivered, kept safe, healed, or made whole. The word *saved* doesn't just apply to our eternal salvation; its implications are so much larger. *Saved* means being made whole and complete—spiritually, mentally, and physically—both in heaven and in this life.

Think about it for a moment. If you asked Jesus to be your best friend, invited him into your heart, and made him Lord of your life, you would be saved. That's the word we use for this decision, and for this experience. It's a good word to use for this because it's true. But how many of us have limited the interpretation of *saved* to mean we are no longer going to hell when we die? That's not the definition Paul meant when he wrote that verse in Romans.

The fact is, we don't need to be delivered, healed, or rescued once we get to heaven. Those needs don't exist there. Salvation, in every aspect of its definition, is for the here and now. We have access to the gospel of salvation through the love that is Jesus. That's why it's called "the good news." It truly is an all-encompassing, life-changing revelation.

The belief that Jesus loves us leads us to salvation and strengthens us with power that is the love of God. His goodness, grace, mercy, hope, justice, peace, and joy are available to us regardless of life's circumstances. That's good news!

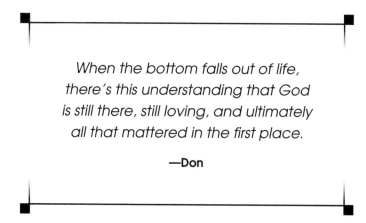

When the bottom falls out of life,
there's this understanding that God
is still there, still loving, and ultimately
all that mattered in the first place.

—Don

Closing Thoughts

Is it possible that the love of God has the power to provide for every need you have? If so, in what way might you engage his love today?

What are some areas in your life that you have kept separate from God? How can you begin to allow God access into those areas?

Small Group Discussion Questions

These questions will be discussed at your small group meeting.

1. *What comes to mind when you hear the phrase "the love of God"?*

1

WEEK

What are your thoughts on the difference between believing in and actually experiencing the love of God?

2. *God has a unique and special love for you. He says that you are "the one he loves." In what areas of life do you struggle with receiving God's love, and why?*

In what areas can you choose to say yes and believe God's love?

3. Have there been times in your life when God's love seemed more apparent than it was in others? Explain what that was like.

1

When have you experienced being forgiven by someone you offended?

When have you experienced forgiving someone else who didn't necessarily deserve it?

4. *What spiritual, emotional, or physical needs do you have today? Have you asked God to meet them? If not, why?*

Do you feel there are certain things you need but that you don't have the right to ask for? If so, what are they? And what is your reason behind this belief?

1

5. *How often do you judge others or yourself based on their ability to follow the "rules" of Christianity?*

When you fail to meet the perceived "rules" of Christianity, how does that affect the way you relate to God?

6. *Are there areas of your life that you feel make you unworthy of God's love? What are they?*

Why do these areas make you feel unworthy, and who taught you to feel this way?

Jesus is the only one worthy of love, but he died so we may be worthy of love. What feeling or emotion does that stir in you?

How Do We Interact with God?

Opening Thoughts

- Have you been taught that you are supposed to interact with God in certain ways or by using certain words?

- What words do you use when you describe God? How do you think of him as he relates to you?

- Do you have a special place you go to feel close to God?

■ Day 1: So Worth the Blood of Jesus

Did you know that not only does God love us, but he likes us? Humans were his idea and he only has good ideas. In fact, in the history of God, he has never, not once, not ever, made a mistake. God is also fully aware of what it's like to not have you and me around because he existed before he created us. It's safe to say he clearly likes it better with us here. Need proof? Just look in a mirror.

At no point has God been surprised by what has taken place on earth—not when Adam and Eve sinned and not even when I barked, "Hurry up, Grandma!" at the guy driving so painfully slow in front of me this morning. God exists outside of time, allowing him to see both beginning and end. Therefore, he has never wondered if maybe we are a lost cause. He has never been discouraged or lost hope or questioned our worth.

So why is it that I often feel as though God is disappointed with me? Why do I often feel like a lost cause? There are lies that have been going around ever since Adam first sinned, and they sound a little something like this: "You aren't special; you are prone to do wrong; you are one step away from evil; you are not good or righteous or holy; you are worthless; you are a lost cause."

If humanity really were a lost cause, what Jesus did on the cross would have been a tragic waste of time. The fact is, God doesn't create junk, and Jesus wouldn't die for a worthless cause. You only die for something you love. So Jesus came. He was love displayed in human form. He was beaten and faced the cross. He did it as love, and for love, he became sin—Adam's, yours, and mine.

Even though it may sound shocking, we are so worth the blood of Jesus. He died so that we could be restored back to our original value. That is to say, God finds us valuable enough to give up his Son's life in order to redeem us to a relationship with him. God not only loves us, he takes joy in relationship with us. He isn't only interested in being our God; he wants to be our best friend as well. He likes us.

Hebrews 12:2 says that "for the joy set before him (Jesus) endured the cross." Has it ever crossed your mind that *you* are that joy? On his way to the cross, Jesus looked into the future and saw you. He knew his death and resurrection would deliver you from an empty religion into a rich relationship. And that's always been the plan—a fully restored relationship with God.

There have been times in my life when I have experienced feelings of worthlessness. But I am learning that truth is not always found in a feeling or a thought. Truth is always found in love. Years ago, I decided I would start seeing myself as God sees me. Not only that, I would begin to interact with God from his perspective—that I am worth all his effort. I am not worthless . . . God's love has made sure of that.

2
WEEK

> *Every day I want to hear from God. Every morning I pray, "God, you lead me and guide me through this day and everything I think and say and do, you lead me and guide me. Make me know your will and help me to do it."*
>
> **—Kathryn**

Closing Thoughts

Is it possible that you truly are "so worth the blood of Jesus"? If so, what does that change regarding your understanding of who you can become in Jesus?

God often works through other people and circumstances. What are some instances in your life that you can look back on and see God working in your favor?

■ Day 2: God's Love Language

God is always speaking to us. John 16:13 says, "But when he, the Spirit of truth, comes, he will guide you into all truth. He will not speak on his own; he will speak only what he hears, and he will tell you what is yet to come." If we ask God into our heart, we enter into a daily relationship with his Holy Spirit known as "the Spirit of truth." When God's Holy Spirit of truth dwells in our hearts, we have the capacity to interact with God. Not only can he hear us, but we can also hear him.

One day as I was driving home, I began to sing an old song. Though I hadn't heard it in years, it came to mind while I had been praying that morning, and it just stayed with me through-out the day. As I sang, the lyrics—which sang of lifting our voices to worship the Lord, to please him with what he hears from us—captivated me.

I kept singing the last two lines, as it was truly my heart's cry that my life would be a sweet, sweet sound to God's ears. I real-ized how I have been given love beyond measure, and my heart was overwhelmed by the goodness of God in my life, even in the midst of hardship. His love has always been a sweet, sweet sound to my ears, and I couldn't help but want to be that for him as well.

After a few minutes of my solo performance, I decided to turn on the radio, and the exact song I had been singing was playing. It was a small, sweet reminder of how God speaks to me in his own language.

This Christian journey is about a relationship with God—a day-in, day-out walk with God. And in a relationship, communication is vitally important. God is always speaking to us. And he always takes joy in our pursuit, desiring for us to have familiarity with how he speaks and how he reveals his presence in our lives.

When you love someone, you learn to speak their language. Learning how God speaks to me is probably the most meaningful thing I will ever do. And no matter how he speaks, I want to hear him. So I've learned that it's very important to have good sources: the Bible, friends, family, and godly teachers. But mostly, I want to hear him in that still, small voice that speaks to my heart and, sometimes, even to my ears.

I go for a walk at five o'clock in the morning. It's my alone time where I just talk to God as if he's walking next to me. I pray over my family and different things that are going on and things I'm struggling with or things I'm very happy about.

—Tae

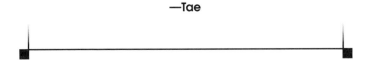

Closing Thoughts

How have you recently heard God? Take a moment and ask the Holy Spirit to reveal God's unique love language for you.

Do you take the time throughout your day to slow down and just be still? Often, that's the time when we can hear God speak. If you don't have a habit of taking some time out each day, what are some ways you can include even five or ten minutes of solitude in your daily routine?

■ Day 3: A Pure Heart

Years ago I received a demo from a guy who had written and recorded five songs. I am a singer/songwriter and a worship leader, so this happens occasionally. He wanted my thoughts on his project. Now, I am no critic, and I don't ever want to be one. I will always look for something I can celebrate in another person—but this five-song demo stretched me.

I didn't want to crush his dreams, but he needed melodic healing. In other words, singing just wasn't his thing. So I began to converse with God in my heart. "God, what can I share with this guy regarding his songs that would encourage his heart in you?" Immediately I had a memory.

Years earlier, this same guy had visited a Bible study group I was a part of. During the worship time, he sang with passion, his eyes closed, and his arms extended. This guy loved God, and he loved to worship him. After this memory, God spoke to my heart. It was as though he was saying, "A man could write a beautiful song with well-crafted lyrics, an incredible chorus with amazing biblical truth. He could have the voice of an angel and the musical gifting to go along. He could record it with a million-dollar budget in the best studio in the world. But if he did not sing it with the sincere, pure heart that this man has when he worships me, then it would not bless me. I listen with different ears. I hear the heart of a man, and I find this man's songs beautiful!"

God has never been concerned with our level of talent or natural gifting, and he has never been worried by our insufficiencies. He is fully sufficient. What God seeks in us is sincerity. He desires a pure relationship, free of hypocrisy or fear. I believe that the enemy of sincerity is hypocrisy. I also think hypocrisy is something that God really dislikes. When you see Jesus rebuke someone in the Bible, it's almost always a hypocrite.

Plus, God has different ears than we do. His ears are tuned to hear far beyond our talent—or lack thereof. God hears sincerity and it pleases him like no other sound. What's amazing is that when we come to God with a sincere, pure, authentic heart, he shows up. As Matthew 5:8 says, "Blessed are the pure in heart, for they will see God."

To interact with God, we simply come to him with a sincere heart. We surrender all our strengths for his and come as we are. If we want to learn how to hear God, and how to see him in our daily lives, it starts with a sincerity of heart.

What God saw in my singing friend was a sincere expression of worship, and that is something that will always bless his heart. I told my friend to keep writing and singing love songs to Jesus. He may not win a Grammy, but the amazing life God will release in and through him because of his sincere worship is something the world not only needs but also longs to hear.

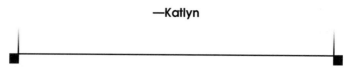

I have a very short attention span and I found that when I close my eyes to pray, I fall asleep. I journal a lot. I'm more of a cerebral thinker so it helps for me to journal things out.

—Katlyn

Closing Thoughts

Is there an area in your life where you need to remove your mask with God? Write your own love song to Jesus. Sing it to him in the shower or driving down the road. He wants your heart, and he wants to give you his.

Maybe you're not a singer or a writer. But you certainly have a talent. Have you discovered it yet? How can you use your talent to praise God?

■ Day 4: The Holy Spirit

I am fully convinced that this journey we are on is not possible outside of a daily relationship with God. And when I say God, I mean God in all of his "God-ness." That may be a new term, so stick with me. I am referring to the triune God; God as three in one. He is our heavenly Father, he is the Son (Jesus), and he is the Holy Spirit.

When it comes to having a relationship with God, I think it's possible to understand him as a father. Even if we have had poor fathers or none at all, we can all understand the concept at least. Jesus is also relatively easy to grasp because he actually walked the earth as flesh and blood. He ate and laughed and experienced all of our emotions. He was a human being, something to which we can obviously relate.

The Holy Spirit, though, is a bit tougher to get our arms around— literally. For one thing, he is a spirit. It's hard to understand what you can't see, and the Holy Spirit clearly falls into that category. Acts 2:2 refers to the Holy Spirit as wind. With wind, you know it's there. You can see evidence when it blows through the trees and you can feel it on your face, but you can't actually see it.

We live in a day when seeing is believing. But on this journey with God, if you think about it, it's actually the other way around. Believing is seeing. And when it comes to the Holy Spirit, it starts with believing—believing that we are meant to interact with not just part of God but all of God.

The Bible is pretty clear regarding the Holy Spirit. He is meant to be an integral part of our journey with God. Second Corinthians 13:14 says, "The grace of the Lord Jesus Christ, and the love of God, and the fellowship of the Holy Spirit be with you all." Our relationship with the Holy Spirit is described here as a fellowship, and if we want to grow or mature in our faith, if we want to keep moving forward in our God story, we don't have the option of knowing part of God. We must know all of him: the Father, the Son, and the Holy Spirit. And here's why.

During the three years of his public ministry, Jesus spent some quality time with his disciples. Of all humanity, these men knew Jesus best. At least, they knew him within the human parameters that we can easily understand. So when Jesus rose from the dead and met with them, they probably couldn't wait to pick up where they left off.

But Jesus knew the plan from the beginning, and he told the disciples it was actually better for them if he ascend to heaven and the Holy Spirit come in his place. In John 16:7 Jesus said, "But I tell you the truth: It is for your good that I am going away. Unless I go away, the Counselor will not come to you; but if I go, I will send him to you." He placed higher importance on the Holy Spirit coming than him sticking around in earthly form.

That was always the plan. Jesus' death and resurrection bought for us the opportunity of a relationship with God. And this relationship was to be implemented through the Counselor, the Holy Spirit. So when we talk about how to interact with God, we can't ignore the Holy Spirit. The fact is, Jesus died and rose again so we might have relationship, and the Holy Spirit is the means by which we have access to that relationship. I encourage you today to invite the Holy Spirit to reveal himself more fully.

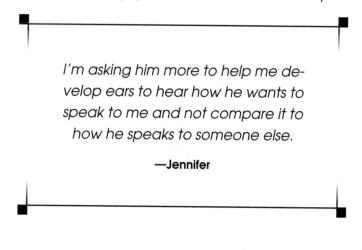

I'm asking him more to help me develop ears to hear how he wants to speak to me and not compare it to how he speaks to someone else.

—Jennifer

Closing Thoughts

How might the Holy Spirit be moving in your heart today? Ask the Holy Spirit to reveal the heart of God to you.

Romans 8:26 says, "In the same way, the Spirit helps us in our weakness. We do not know what we ought to pray for, but the Spirit himself intercedes for us with groans that words cannot express." How does it make you feel to know that the Holy Spirit is constantly helping us to communicate our deepest needs to God?

■ Day 5: No Condemnation

Jesus was walking into Jericho when he saw a little man in a syca-more tree. "Zacchaeus, come on down. I'm coming to your house for dinner," Jesus said. The Bible tells us that Zacchaeus was a bad man and he was also short (not that the two are related). He stole from and cheated the people of Jericho. They didn't like him.

Rather surprisingly, after Zacchaeus met with Jesus, Zacchaeus gave half of what he owned to the poor and returned to those from whom he stole four times more than the amount he had orig-inally taken. Jesus didn't ask him to do this. Jesus didn't even raise his eyebrow and give Zacchaeus the universal parent-look that says, "You know what you need to do." The Bible doesn't always give inflection, but I'm pretty sure Jesus didn't say, "I must eat at your house today" with sarcasm and eye rolling. If there was emphasis on the "must," it was pure enthusiasm.

I have heard this story since I was a child, and I can still sing the cute little ditty about Zacchaeus being "a wee little man." But as a kid without any sense of economics, I thought nothing of the fact that Zacchaeus gave away half his worth. It seemed pretty natural to just give up more than half of what you had because Jesus was nice. It wasn't until I was an adult that I realized I had so much in common with the story of Zacchaeus.

Jesus comes and honors me by meeting with me. He doesn't bring up my past, my weakness, or my failures. There is no condem-nation, shame, or guilt. Instead, when I find myself in his presence, I am simply humbled by his love for me. Yes, I am aware of who I am but I am infinitely more aware of who he is and that he dwells in me. Because of his overwhelming love, my heart is challenged to be holy as he is holy.

I know Zacchaeus's generosity wasn't inspired just because Jesus was nice. Nice is, well, nice, but it doesn't have the power to inspire all that Zacchaeus ended up doing. This wasn't just about Jesus being nice. This was about Zacchaeus experiencing the rev-elation of Jesus' love in the form of unmerited grace and mercy.

Once Jesus' love is encountered, life changes. Once Jesus' love is received, we are changed and we can't go on living as we once did. Love is what pricks a conscience. Love is what *convicts* us.

It is important to remember that there is a difference between conviction and condemnation. It is Jesus' *love* that convicts us, and it is his love that releases the power of mercy and grace. One is holy and the other is evil. One brings life, the other death. When I meet with Jesus, I never come away feeling condemned. That's not how he operates. It is actually counter to his nature. If somehow you are experiencing shame or condemnation when you meet with God, you didn't get those feelings from him. They were probably there before you met with him, and instead of giving those burdens to him, you held on and took them away with you.

What we think about ourselves should always be determined by what God thinks about us. We should want to see ourselves through his eyes. In God's eyes, Zacchaeus wasn't a small-minded, selfish, thieving liar; he was a generous, big-hearted believer who was capable of giving away more than half of what he owned. Zacchaeus's response to Jesus' love was to extend the same generosity to those around him—especially to those he'd wronged. When we see ourselves through God's eyes, we become capable of all the things that condemnation says we aren't.

> *When I look back at my life, I'm astounded and in awe of the gentleness of God and how he has painstakingly created circumstances and brought people into my life to influence it and to set me free.*
>
> **—Rogan**

Closing Thoughts

What condemnation are you holding on to?

What are you allowing to come between God and yourself?
Give it to him today.

Small Group Discussion Questions

These questions will be discussed at your small group meeting.

1. *God didn't give his Son unto death for lost causes. We are so worth the blood of Jesus. What does it mean to you that you are made in the image of God?*

What does it mean to you that your neighbor, your co-worker, your best friend, and even your worst enemy are made in the image of God?

2. *God enjoys you. He invites you to also take joy in him by learning more of who he is and about his love language for you. How can you be intentional every day about developing your love language skills with God?*

Some people keep journals, some people say silent prayers to God during the day, and some people have scheduled times in their days to be alone with God. Everyone is different and there's not a wrong answer. How do you prefer to talk to God?

2

WEEK

3. *God desires pure worship from a surrendered heart. When we live this way toward him, he reveals his heart to us in greater measure. In what area of life would you like to see God?*

What are some dreams and goals you have? Where is God in the midst of those hopes? Have you let God into those areas of your life? What would it look like to surrender those things to him?

4. God's Holy Spirit is living inside each believer. God's love language is actually found through "the Spirit of truth." What has been your experience with the Holy Spirit?

How do you understand the role of the Holy Spirit in your relationship with God?

5. Looking back on your life, when may it have occurred that God was speaking to you all along, even if you didn't realize it at the time?

2

WEEK

6. *In what ways have you let condemnation separate you from God's love?*

In what ways have you let condemnation separate you from the love of others?

the
opentable vol. 2
an invitation to **walk** with God

Does God Care about Community?

WEEK 3

Opening Thoughts

- Think about ways you have seen communities rally together in times of need. What causes have you been a part of?
- Who in your life have you looked up to as a mentor?
- Have you ever considered being a mentor for someone else?

■ Day 1: A Culture of Honor

When I was younger, one of my favorite songs was one about the hope that people would be able to recognize Christians by the way we show love. It seemed so powerful—the idea that a believer could be known by how he or she loves. And even though growing up introduced me to many unloving "Christians," I'm still convinced that the true marker for the church is to become love.

But church is not a building down the street. It's not a religion or a set of beliefs. Church is not an idea or a state of mind. If we ask Jesus into our hearts, we choose to be loved and to become love. The becoming love part, well, that's called church. Church is you and me choosing to love Jesus together. Unfortunately, the word *church* is often relegated to describe an institutional idea regarding a community. This is not completely incorrect; church *is* a community, but it is so much more than an institution.

59

Jesus was the first church. He was the first community. In fact, church is perfectly revealed in the person of Jesus Christ. The Bible says that Jesus did only what he saw his heavenly Father doing (John 5:19). It also says the Holy Spirit and Jesus are in perfect agreement (John 16:13). I'm convinced that this perfect love-community Jesus has with his heavenly Father and the Holy Spirit is the model for church. And this community, this love relationship, was defined by one principle—honor.

If you look at the relationship Jesus had with his heavenly Father and the Holy Spirit, you will see that in everything, love is always expressed through honor. Jesus knew how to honor, and this was shown not only in how he interacted with his heavenly Father and the Holy Spirit but also in how he loved those around him.

In his time on earth, there was something beautiful about the way Jesus interacted with people. Throughout the Gospels we read of a Jesus who, when looking at a person, saw double. What I mean by this is that he saw both who they were and who they could become in him.

Let's look at Zacchaeus again for a moment. Jesus honored Zacchaeus by stopping by for dinner. Jesus saw double—he looked past Zacchaeus's transgressions and chose to honor the man Zacchaeus *could* be. In so doing, Jesus gave Zacchaeus the grace he needed in order to step into his full potential in God. Zacchaeus went on to give half of what he owned to the poor.

If you are concerned that this kind of honor ignores sin, the opposite is actually true. This kind of honor convicts a heart to sincere repentance and releases a believer into his or her full potential.

It is my prayer that we would begin to develop a culture of honor within our hearts whereby we are able to see double. I hope that we might see people the way Jesus does and there-fore celebrate the gift of God within them. It is my prayer that we would begin to bless the potential of who a person can become in Christ while celebrating their unique gifts and personality. When we treat people this way—with honor—it not only releases grace upon them to step into their God-given potential, it also frees us to love in new and greater ways.

There is something so amazing about this truth. If we, "the church," could better honor and celebrate Jesus in each other, we could enter such a revelation of community that the world would truly know us by our love.

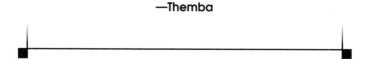

I saw a lot of hypocrisy in people around me and even in my own life. The Bible was starting to become more of a fable, just good stories and good morals, and not something that was really living and active and true. When I got to college, I came in contact with a really incredible guy who started to model for me that real Christianity was livable.

—Themba

Closing Thoughts

Who can you choose to honor in your heart today? How can you better celebrate those around you, regardless of differences?

List some ways you can help people today, no matter how small those actions may seem.

■ Day 2: No Man Is an Island

The word *community* has an incredibly broad connotation. It can be applied to both a small group and a global network. We have art communities, retirement communities, and church communities. There are community colleges and community centers. The word can mean one thing to one person and something entirely different to another. However, regardless of connotation, most of us like the word—it stirs our hearts and it seems good.

I love the movie *About a Boy*. Hugh Grant plays a man who claims to have life all figured out. The movie opens with a voice-over of Grant's character telling us how to live a contented life. "In my opinion, all men are islands," he says. He then goes on to wax eloquently about how he is an island, how he doesn't need anyone, how this makes him happy, and how Swedish women find this attractive.

This monologue sets the tone for our introduction to a self-centered guy who has intentionally sought to live a purposeless life filled with the trivial and the superficial. Grant's character is a man who avoids inconvenience at all costs, especially when it comes to relationships. As far as he is concerned, relationships are the standard bearer for inconvenience.

The reason the movie works, the reason I love it, and the reason it is a good story, is because even the most "John Wayne" of us know the truth—mankind was made for community. The fact is, a need for relationship is in our DNA; it's how we were created. At the very beginning of the book of Genesis, we read about an Adam who was lonely. God created Adam with a need and then stated: "It is not good for the man to be alone" (Genesis 2:18).

Adam was designed for relationship, first with God and then with another. So it is in us, this need to be in relationship. And I believe that's why we love the word *community*. We apply it in so many ways because it's something we are always searching for.

In the movie, Grant's character, stuck in empty selfishness, stumbles across an opportunity for community. He learns that community is both wonderful and messy. It's both appealing and disquieting, and above all, it's extremely inconvenient. Finally, he is forced to make a decision: either he will continue on as an island or he will surrender the island for community. In the end, he surrenders his comforts, his affections, his pride, and ultimately his trust. The last line of the movie resolves by correcting the first line to "*no* man is an island." And we viewers feel good because we know in our gut it's true and that Hugh Grant's character is better off than when we first found him.

It is true that no man is an island. We were created to be known and to know God, and we were created to be known and to know each other. A true community is built on authentic relationships. And here's the amazing thing: not only are we created for community, but God has given incredible life to those who seek community.

As we begin to love each other, all the wonderful benefits of community come to bear in our lives. When we enter into a community, we have access to each other's strengths and to the power of God's love. Matthew 18:20 tells us that wherever two

or more believers are gathered, God shows up in the power of heaven. Essentially, a community has a greater capacity to positively impact not only the lives of each other but also the greater world around us. When true community happens, we have access to greater love and every aspect of love becomes more available to us.

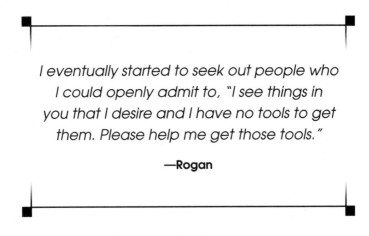

I eventually started to seek out people who I could openly admit to, "I see things in you that I desire and I have no tools to get them. Please help me get those tools."

—Rogan

Closing Thoughts

Is there any part of your life in which you have chosen "island" living? If so, how might you begin to get off the island?

*If you have family or friends who have this "island" mentality,
how can you begin to reach out to them?*

■ Day 3: Mentors

Just as we were made for community, we also were designed
with both a need to be mentored and to mentor. This mentor
relationship fits inside of community. I have had some amazing
mentors over the course of my life—men and women who have
played wonderfully important roles. They have encouraged and
challenged me into a greater revelation regarding my identity
in Christ and greatly influenced me for the work of the kingdom.
Dick Grout is one of those men. Dick was the worship director of
the local Bible college. He is a quiet man, humble and patient,
and he loves God.

For three hours every Monday night, I would go to a Servant
meeting. "Servant" was the name of the student worship ministry
Dick led. The Servant group would go out a few times a semester
to churches in the surrounding area. During those Monday night
meetings, we would prepare for the upcoming trip and Dick would
encourage us to lean into Jesus and to learn how to hear from

God. On the weekends out, we experienced incredible opportunities to serve the church, the community, and each other. During that season of life, Dick played the role of mentor and it was a precious thing.

Through serving us, Dick modeled what it was to be in a love relationship with God. He honored us through the giving of his time. He challenged and encouraged us to love Jesus more. The true role of a mentor is to lead a person into a greater understanding of who they are in Christ. Looking back on that time, I now realize that Dick's one goal in mentoring us was that we would become more like Jesus.

After all, Jesus, the perfect example of community, is also the perfect example of a mentor. For three years, Jesus mentored twelve men on a daily basis. During those three years, Jesus had one purpose with his disciples—he was all about reproducing himself in them.

The Bible makes it clear that the journey of a believer is about becoming like Jesus. Romans 8:29 tells us to "be conformed to the likeness of his Son," and in 2 Corinthians 3:18 we read that we "are being transformed into (Jesus') likeness with ever-increasing glory." A mentor is someone who leads a believer into a greater revelation regarding who they are becoming in Christ.

You can find mentors in every aspect of life. They are fathers and mothers, sisters and brothers. They are friends and teachers. They are athletes and artists. They wait tables and they perform surgery. Mentoring is not just the job of pastors, and it's not a Christian occupation. A mentor is a person who is marked by love, and who inspires that love in another person.

In community, we are designed to receive and to give. Again, we are loved and we are becoming love. This means we are meant to both be mentored and mentor others. I am on this planet for two reasons: to be loved and to leave a legacy of love. That's why you are here as well.

WEEK

> *It's always good to have people who will encourage you when you're feeling discouraged . . . It feels really great to know that you are helping someone get closer to God.*

—Marcia

Closing Thoughts

If you don't currently have a mentor, think of someone you know whose life is a great example of the life you'd like to live. What is it about this person that makes him or her a great example?

Would you be willing to seek out a mentor? Why or why not?

■ Day 4: The Presence

When I bought my house, it was late fall and most of the leaves had fallen off the trees. Everything was bare. When spring arrived the trees started to bud and it was then that I noticed my neighbor's tree was dead. During the winter, it looked like every other tree in the neighborhood, but once spring hit, it stood in stark contrast to the life all around me.

Regardless of species, trees all have one thing in common: the first sign of life is always the budding leaf. Some trees go on to produce tastier fruits like apples or walnuts, but the first fruit of a tree is its leaves. In John 15:5, Jesus said, "I am the vine; you are the branches. If a man remains in me and I in him, he will bear much fruit; apart from me you can do nothing."

The vine, God, is always about producing life. In fact, Jesus refers to himself as "life" in John 14:6. So it's pretty straightforward: a love relationship with God will bear fruit. And if we engage God's love, we enter into a fruit-bearing life. If we say yes to love, we are saying yes to life.

So what does this life look like? Well, it's green and leafy and sometimes there are apples or walnuts. In other words, life is really about fruit, and we can see that another scripture in the Bible uses the metaphor of fruit to talk about what a community looks like when it is truly alive. Galatians 5:22–23 says that "the fruit of the Spirit is love, joy, peace, patience, kindness, goodness, faithfulness, gentleness and self-control."

When we look for a community to make our own, and when we seek mentors, brothers, and sisters to live the journey with, we are looking for a people marked by God's presence. When I look for a community, I want to know that we are pursuing the same thing—God's presence. Of course, I'm not saying we have to agree on everything. True community is not about conformity but about being transformed into the image of Christ.

If you want to know what God's presence looks like in a community, look for evidence of the fruit of his Spirit. The Holy Spirit is the revealed presence of God, and it always looks like love, joy, peace, patience, kindness, goodness, faithfulness, gentleness, and self-control. These are the attributes of a love community, and they give us practical mile markers for what community is meant to look like.

It's all relational. The stuff of heaven is about the exchange of love and we get to experience that in a very small percentage here on earth in the form of community.

—Don

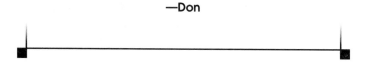

Closing Thoughts

In what area of your life might you ask God to reveal his presence so you could bear more fruit?

*What exactly would you want that fruit to look like? Do you
desire to be more caring? more patient? more disciplined? How
do you envision your life changing as a result of bearing more
fruit in these areas?*

■ Day 5: Dangerous Love

Jennifer had gone to church her whole life. She enjoyed the people, and for the most part she enjoyed the sermons, but during
her junior year in college, she started to wonder if that's all church
was—a group of people who met once a week in a building to
sing off key and listen to a man talk about God. She was becoming disenchanted with religion, to say the least.

Since she had left home to go to school, she had noticed
more of her surroundings. She realized that not everyone had a
mom and dad who loved them. She saw families who lived just off
campus who didn't look as though they had much of anything.
Young, single moms with two or three kids. Older couples whose
family had forgotten about them.

Jennifer started to wonder, *If God loves me, why doesn't he appear to love them?* One Sunday after church she decided to buy groceries and head over to the homeless camp across town. She didn't know exactly what they'd need—bread, cans of ravioli, water—but she filled a few bags and headed over.

She didn't know what to expect, and she didn't even know what to say. She just knew that these people needed food. As she walked toward a group of men, she kept repeating the verse in her head from Matthew 25:40: "The King will reply, 'I tell you the truth, whatever you did for one of the least of these brothers of mine, you did for me.'"

She was not but twenty steps away when she began to wonder if this was a bad idea. Most of the men ignored her, but some were already heckling and whistling at her. She timidly walked up to the group and said, "I brought you some food. I didn't know what you might need but I hope this helps." One older man walked up and took the bags from her, and a few of the other guys started laughing. She felt confused and ashamed and turned around to go back to her car. As she did, one man said, "Thank you."

She was crying as she drove back to her dorm room but decided she would go back next week with a group of friends and more food.

This time when she walked up to the camp with bags of food, they didn't laugh at her. A few of the guys who came with Jennifer started to talk to the men and listened to their stories. Some of the guys had been in jail. Some had lost jobs. Some had lost families over addictions. But they were all likeable. And they all felt like outcasts. Their little homeless camp was the only bit of community they had.

Over the next two semesters, Jennifer and her group continued to bring food to the men every week. They also started talking to them about the love of God. They became the love in action that John 13:34 talks about: "Just as I have loved you, you also are to love one another" (ESV).

The change in the men was amazing. Two of them found steady work and one man reunited with his family. But the experience changed Jennifer too. She looked forward to Sundays and she sought out more ways to help others. Most importantly, she realized that God did love everyone and that oftentimes, he loved *through* people.

Jesus and the disciples are the best example of a community that loved dangerously. They loved the outcasts. They healed the sick. They gave hope to the hopeless and they taught others that love received is not fully realized until it is given away.

The disciples showed us what happens when a community understands that the love of God is the most radical thing this world will know. His love heals, restores, and redeems. All the strengths of salvation and all the fruits of the Spirit are evidenced in the love of God through the community of believers.

> *He doesn't just want us to be in a Christian community. I think he wants us to have a wide community where we're interacting with people from different nations and different social and economic statuses. He wants us to cross lines in community and that's what Jesus was always doing. He was always reaching over to people who were different from him.*
>
> **—Megan**

Closing Thoughts

So many times we don't notice people in our presence who could use a little encouragement. Is there someone you know who might be in need? What could you do to help him or her?

Is there some place in your life where you can step out of your comfort zone and show love to those who desperately need to feel it?

Small Group Discussion Questions

These questions will be discussed at your small group meeting.

1. What is your definition of community?

What good things come to mind when you think about community?

What negative associations do you have with the idea of community?

2. *There are two types of surrender: one is by force and the other is voluntary. God has never forced surrender. That's not how love works. So when we come to God we choose to surrender. And that is always the key to any good love relationship.*

   Community is God's idea. We cannot make it alone. We are not designed that way. How can you become intentional regarding your surrender that you might step away from "island living"?

List two specific ways you can think of that you can involve yourself more in your community.

3. God's perfect community—the Trinity—is grounded in love. The perfect love between them is revealed through how they honor first each other, and then us. How can we begin to live from this principle in our lives regarding:

Our family

Our friends and neighbors

Our church

Everyone we meet

4. Mentoring is a profound relationship within the context of community. These relationships bring believers into a greater understanding of their identity in Christ. In the area of mentoring, how can you begin to receive and to give?

You don't have to be old and wise to be a mentor. No matter who you are or what your life experience has been, you have some very powerful lessons to teach right now. Over the past year, can you think of one good lesson or profound experience you've had that you could share with others? Share that lesson.

5. *Is your community living and loving dangerously? In what ways?*

Where can you begin to take steps to get out of your comfort zone?

6. *God's presence is the most important aspect of a love community. In what areas do you see or not see the fruit of God's presence in your community?*

If you do see God's presence in your community, how can you be a part of that? If you don't see his presence, how can you begin to change that?

What Does Faith Look Like?

Opening Thoughts

- Have you ever taken risks in your life? How did they turn out?

- Are there areas in your life now in which you are struggling to walk through by faith?

- Are you able to trust God with your every decision and every situation? If not, what fears are you holding on to?

■ Day 1: God Is Always Good

In the first chapter, I noted that God is always saying to us, "I love you," and this statement is always followed up by the question, "Do you believe me?"

The Bible says that without faith we cannot please God (Hebrews 11:16). Another word for faith is belief. God's one passion, his one desire, his one dream is that we would believe that his love for us is beyond imagining; that we would exhibit faith in the absolute goodness of his love. That's what faith is—believing that God is good, that he loves us, and then living without fear.

It's risky, this thing called faith. It's risky because God has invited us to believe and act on the goodness of his love even though we live in a messy world. We are invited to believe even when we experience hurts and heartaches. We are invited to believe in the midst of pain, challenges, disappointments, and failure. Regardless of our circumstances, God is always inviting us to step out and believe. Believing is faith in action, and it always looks like risk.

Taking risks means that we will fail occasionally. And sometimes what we plan doesn't work out. Sometimes our best efforts aren't enough. Sometimes we get it wrong. The fact is, God isn't interested in fail-safe plans. He doesn't wring his hands when life blows up in our faces, and he doesn't get nervous when our grand gestures fall flat. Why? It's because he knows the end of every story, and as Roman 8:28 says, "In *all things* God works for the good of those who *love* him, who have been called according to his purpose" (emphasis mine).

This scripture tells us that the gospel we have been invited to live has its foundations in the goodness of God's love. Believing the truth of God's good love is the cornerstone of a Christian's true identity; it is what this journey is all about; and it also implies great risk. Once we have secured in our hearts the goodness of God's love, we begin to become transformed into that same love . . . the same love that led Jesus to a wilderness and, later, the cross.

It's important to know that when we choose to walk with Jesus, we are being love and becoming love, and this will often lead us into risk. On this journey, for the sake of love, we will experience pain, disappointments, challenges, failures, and loss. Like Jesus we will have both wilderness experiences and cross experiences. But this gospel we are living is called the Good News for a reason. It comes with a promise that God will work it all out for our good. In the end, the risk of believing in the goodness of God's love always pays off.

Granted, a life with Jesus is not always safe—at least not in the typical sense of the word. A journey with Jesus is often hard, sometimes scary, and even death defying. But it's also a miracle upon miracle and a life-giving adventure—at least that's how Jesus lived it. Becoming a Christian doesn't make life easy; it just opens up the possibility of becoming like Jesus. It's an invitation to finding our identity in Christ.

4

WEEK

Loving the way Jesus loves is dangerous and beautiful. It's scary and rarely easy, and at the same time, it's inspiring and fulfilling. There are signs and wonders and miracles at every turn. We have been invited to join a good God on a journey filled with risk and miracles. It's a journey that can only be engaged to the extent that we know without a doubt he is good and his love will never fail us (1 Corinthians 13:8).

Faith for me is stepping off a cliff and not really knowing where you're going to fall or if you're going to crash, but being completely trusting that God's going to catch you.

—Tim

Closing Thoughts

In what area of life might you risk believing in the always-good love of God?

Sometimes we fail to have faith because we can't possibly see how a situation will turn out well. Have you experienced situations like this before? How did they turn out?

■ Day 2: Identity

Everyone loves a good story. But beyond reading, hearing, or watching a great story, I think every person, deep down, has the desire to *live* a good story. We desire to live stories filled with love, wonder, and promise—a story that is inspired and will inspire others. In thinking about story, there are two elements common to a good story. First, the best stories end well. And second, before they end "happily ever after," they are filled with conflict, risk, and sometimes even death.

Jesus lived a great—no, the greatest—story. His was full of wonder and mercy and love and friendship. But it was also filled with conflict and risk, even unto death. And if there was a crisis in his story, it was a crisis of identity. Not with Jesus himself—he never doubted who he was—but those around him certainly did. If you think about it, the question of Jesus' identity followed him everywhere he went.

Jesus was actually born into a crisis of identity. As far as public perception was concerned, his birth was a little sketchy. His inception was miraculous. He was born of a virgin. Scripture refers to him as "God with us" (Matthew 1:23) and "The Son of God" (Luke 1:35). However, that part of Scripture was unavailable at the time of Jesus, as it hadn't been written yet. Most likely, Jesus grew up with the stigma of the seemingly scandalous circumstances of his birth. He was born out of wedlock as his earthly father, Joseph, waited until after his birth to wed Jesus' mother, Mary. But Jesus was not insecure. He knew who he was.

We know this because of the one story we have of Jesus in his youth. When he was twelve, Jesus and his family journeyed to Jerusalem. When they left for home, his parents did not realize he had not come with them, and for three days they searched for him throughout Jerusalem. They finally found him at the temple. When his mother asked him where he had been, he replied, "Didn't you know I had to be in my Father's house?" (Luke 2:49). Jesus knew he was the Son of God. He was sure in his identity.

If you keep reading the rest of Jesus' story, you will find that everywhere he went his identity was questioned and challenged by religious teachers, entire towns, and government officials. The story of Jesus' life was a daily fight for identity. If his story had an antagonist, it was doubt, better known as unbelief. And each time Jesus was confronted with the doubts about his identity, he chose to believe what God had said about him from the very beginning. He continued to live a story of beauty and wonder. He healed the blind and deaf, lame and mute. He raised the dead and turned water into wine. He walked on water and calmed storms. He gave life to anyone who received him for who he was—the Son of God. In fact, everything Jesus did confirmed that he was God's Son.

The question of identity is the theme not only of Jesus' story but of ours as well. To be honest, my entire life has been a search for identity. Daily I come to a greater understanding of the fact that this faith journey I am on is a battle for who I am in Christ. I am at war with an antagonist known as unbelief. The good news is, because Jesus was sure in his identity, we can also become sure in ours.

God has invited us to believe—to believe that he is love, he works for good on our behalf, and we are his sons and daughters. I am confident that our faith journeys are about deciding daily

to be sure in our identities as children of God. The moment we surrender our life to Jesus, the moment we receive his love, is the moment we step into a new identity. When we believe, not only does Jesus confirm and reveal his identity, but he ultimately wins our identity for us. Jesus rose from the grave and forever answered that question for those who choose to believe. We are sons and daughters of God. We are loved and we are becoming love.

This journey we are on will have its breath in that revelation. Like all good stories, there will be highs and lows, pain and beauty, conflict and resolution. And because of the identity of Jesus, we can be sure in our identity and know that our story will always end well.

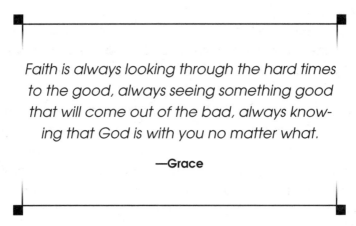

Faith is always looking through the hard times to the good, always seeing something good that will come out of the bad, always knowing that God is with you no matter what.

—Grace

Closing Thoughts

In your story, how sure are you of your identity?

Have you ever questioned your identity? If so, what part did you question, and why? What didn't feel right?

■ Day 3: Even Unto Death

I have a friend from college with whom I have stayed in touch over the years. Along his journey, he met a few hypocrites in the institution of the church. These leaders manipulated truth for their own gain. My friend became offended and eventually he allowed the shortcomings of a few hypocrites to determine his thoughts on God. For a season, he became cynical and angry, and his relationship with God suffered for it.

I have another friend I often meet at a local coffee shop. After a horrible tragedy occurred in his life several years ago, for a season he was distant with God. When we talked about God and his love, it was in theological terms—God's love was real but it wasn't applicable to his journey. This friend had allowed a tragedy to affect his relationship with God.

On this journey of faith, there will be times when we will be challenged regarding the goodness of God's love. There will be people who screw up, hurt, disappoint, and even betray us. There will be seasons of hardship and sadness where we will be hard-pressed to remember that God works it all out for our good. In these moments of betrayal, disappointment, sadness, or failure, we can become tempted to doubt and forget about the always-good love of God.

According to Scripture, no one in history surpasses John the Baptist as a man of God. John had been imprisoned and was facing execution for preaching about the kingdom of God. For a moment, while in prison, John experienced doubt. He questioned God's goodness. So he sent his disciples to Jesus to ask a question about Jesus' identity, which was really about John's identity as well. "When the men came to Jesus, they said, 'John the Baptist sent us to you to ask, "Are you the one who was to come, or should we expect someone else?'" (Luke 7:20). John's life was hanging in the balance and he wanted an assurance that Jesus truly was who he believed him to be—the Son of God.

Jesus didn't answer John's disciples right away. Over the next few hours, he healed all who were brought to him. Then he turned to John's waiting disciples and answered their question: "Go back and report to John what you have seen and heard: The blind receive sight, the lame walk, those who have leprosy are cured, the deaf hear, the dead are raised, and the good news is preached to the poor. Blessed is the man who does not fall away on account of me" (vv. 22–23). After Jesus had sent the messengers away with these encouraging words for John, he then went on to say to the crowd, "I tell you, among those born of women there is no one greater than John" (v. 28).

In so many words, Jesus' message to John was: "Yes, I am who you believe me to be. Now, will you continue to believe in me? Will you continue to believe in my good love even if it means death? Because blessed are those who don't fall away, who aren't offended, who don't stop believing even when their relationship with me gets them into bad situations."

On this faith journey, there are two ways to handle disappointment and hardship. We can stop believing and fall away, or we can choose to believe even when it could mean death. When the tough season is upon us, we will be tempted to doubt the goodness of God's love. This is when we must choose to believe, and that is precisely what faith is. Faith is believing even when our present circumstance is less than ideal and the future is scary. In these seasons, we must be absolutely sure in his good love or we will never have the faith to become love.

John was sure and, for love, John was beheaded.

This thing called faith is no joke. It's not something casually entered into. We must know who we are in Christ. We must be absolutely convinced and intimately aware of God's good love. We must be always certain that this journey with God isn't about death; it's about resurrected life.

The friends I mentioned earlier are on wonderful God journeys. And for a season they got stuck, moving neither forward nor back. For a season, they substituted the good love of God with disappointment, hurt, and sadness. Instead of the painful experiences driving them to a deeper revelation of God's good love, they allowed the hardship to birth doubt and unbelief. Instead of picking up the cross knowing the story always ends happily ever after—with redemption and resurrection—they chose to become offended by the cross and stopped believing.

Believing is faith, and faith is risky, especially in the tough season. It requires us to believe that God is love and that he will work it out for good, even while we acknowledge disappointment, heartache, and sadness. It requires us to keep moving forward regardless of the circumstances into the wonder of God's good love, even unto death.

Faith is spelled R-I-S-K. It's plain and simple. I want to be a risk-taker. I know that it pleases God to be able to believe and then just get out of the boat.

—Jason

Closing Thoughts

Is there a cross in your life where you can choose to believe God is good? Is there a person in your life who is experiencing a difficult season? If so, how can you come alongside and show love to this person?

During the difficult times of your life, were there people who helped you? If so, how did they do so?

■ Day 4: Obedience

God said, "Abraham!"

"Here I am," replied Abraham.

"Take your son, your only son, Isaac, whom you love, and go to the region of Moriah. Sacrifice him there as a burnt offering on one of the mountains I will tell you about" (Genesis 22:2).

Abraham, so familiar with the voice of God, didn't even question it. He simply obeyed. The Bible says, "Abraham got up early in the morning and saddled his donkey. He took two of his young servants and his son Isaac. He had split wood for the burnt offering. He set out for the place God had directed him. On the third day he looked up and saw the place in the distance. Abraham told his two young servants, 'Stay here with the donkey. The boy and I are going over there to worship; then we'll come back to you'" (vv. 3–5 MSG).

Here is a little backstory. Abraham was over one hundred years old. He had followed God's leading around the countryside for most of his life. Early on, God promised Abraham that he and his wife would have a son who would birth a nation. This promised son would be the birth of Abraham's legacy. Over the course of his long life, Abraham's faith was tested time and again. And through it all, the highs and the lows, he chose to believe what God had promised him so long ago. Over those hundred years or so, Abraham learned that, through obedience, God's story always had the best ending. And then God delivered on his promise and Isaac was born.

That's where we find Abraham suddenly being asked to sacrifice his beloved, promised son. At this point in Abraham's story, he had developed such an intimate ear that he was able to hear God even when what God asked seemed counter to everything Abraham knew God to be. Abraham was able to trust and obey, even when it seemed to conflict with everything God had promised.

To be honest, this story has always bothered me. Abraham's life was a shining example of obedient surrender that culminated in the birth of his son. His legacy as a believer was to be fulfilled through Isaac. And then God, whom Abraham had followed his entire life, asked for Isaac back. It doesn't seem to line up. But I have learned from experience that if you walk with God long enough, if you learn surrendered obedience, eventually God will ask you to do something that seems impossible—something

counter to what you understand. But here's the thing: God won't ask of you something he hasn't already released the faith for. The fact is, the moment God asks, he supplies the faith you need in order to obey. And that's truly what obedience is: faith in action.

In this scripture, there is one word that is so very telling. Abraham, who was going up a mountain to sacrifice his son, said, "The boy and I are going over there to worship; then *we'll* come back to you" (Genesis 22:5 MSG, emphasis mine). Abraham was a believer, and he knew a truth about God: God always comes through, and he always works things out for the good of those who love him. Abraham knew that whether God came through while he was walking up the mountain, while he prepared the altar, or after he plunged the knife, he and his boy were both coming back. Abraham was so sure of God's faithfulness, he was so certain that God was in control, that he could obey even the most insane of requests. He knew God always comes through on his promises.

Abraham's life is a story of chasing obedience. Always on the move, never knowing where his foot might land when he lifted it. He spent his life walking in obedience, and along the way he became intimate with the voice of God. For us, on our own journeys with the Lord, obedience will always lead us into greater intimacy with him—greater intimacy and greater faith.

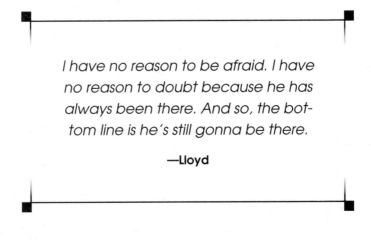

I have no reason to be afraid. I have no reason to doubt because he has always been there. And so, the bottom line is he's still gonna be there.

—Lloyd

Closing Thoughts

Is there an area in your life where you can exhibit faith in God's good love through obedience?

If so, what would that obedience look like?

■ Day 5: Surrendered and Untamed

Gravity is a fact. When I jumped out of an airplane several years ago . . . I fell. I can testify to the truth of gravity. And then there is flight. It is also a fact. It has something to do with wings and aerodynamics, but regardless of the science, before jumping from the plane, I was safely defying gravity. So I can also testify to the truth of flight.

It's true that we fall when we step out of a plane, and it's also true that if we stay in the plane, we fly. Similarly, it's true that a plant needs water to live and it's also true that too much water can kill a plant. This concept is called "truth and tension." One thing being true doesn't mean the other isn't also true. In fact, most truths have a counterpart. And when it comes to our faith journey, there are two primary truths always in tension. There are two ways to express our faith, and though they sound contradictory, they actually work in tandem. We are meant to live a surrendered faith, and we are also meant to live an untamed faith. When we live with faith that is both surrendered and untamed, God's kingdom is engaged, and we experience miracles.

First, let's look at an example of surrendered faith. In Mark 4:37–38, Jesus slept peacefully in a boat while a violent storm raged all around him and his friends, threatening to shipwreck them: "A furious squall came up, and the waves broke over the boat, so that it was nearly swamped. Jesus was in the stern, sleeping on a cushion." Here we see that surrendered faith is a faith found through rest—through a peace that surpasses understanding (Philippians 4:7).

Jesus rested while his treacherous circumstances swirled around him. It was only possible to rest in this situation because he was living a surrendered faith—he was sure in his identity as a *child* of God. Jesus once said, "Let the little children come to me, and do not hinder them, for the kingdom of heaven belongs to such as these" (Matthew 19:14). In other words, God's kingdom is available for those who know how to come to him as a child; those who understand they are God's heirs and can surrender their concerns and simply rest in their identity as sons and daughters.

The story continues with the terrified disciples waking Jesus up. Jesus then spoke to the storm saying, "Peace, be still" (Mark 4:39 KJV). The winds immediately stopped blowing and the seas calmed. And here we see surrendered faith resulting in the miraculous.

Interestingly, an example of untamed faith took place with the disciples once again in a boat during a storm—this time without Jesus. The wind and waves shook the boat and the disciples were terrified, when suddenly they saw Jesus walking on the water. The disciples were afraid and thought they were seeing a ghost, but Peter, one of Jesus' beloved disciples, cried out, "'Lord, if it's you . . . tell me to come to you on the water.' 'Come,' (Jesus) said. Then Peter got down out of the boat, walked on the water and came toward Jesus" (Matthew 14:28–29). In spite of his fear, Peter's wild faith allowed him to take a risk in this situation. Because he was sure of God's good love, Peter was able to do the impossible. His untamed faith resulted in the miraculous, and he literally walked on water.

The Bible shows us that the kingdom of God is engaged through surrendered and untamed believing—two truths held in tension. Our faith journeys inevitably will be marked by these two truths. Sometimes, in the midst of a storm, we will be asked to believe and to rest in our identities as sons or daughters of God. Other times, we will be asked to believe, to be sure in the always-good love of God, and to take great risk as we step out into the middle of a storm. And every time we believe, every time we live with surrendered and untamed faith, God moves upon our lives in miraculous ways.

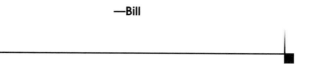

There's no doubt that when you see the fruit of your faith, it's a tremendous encouragement. But even when you make a mistake, it's never a mistake to trust God because he causes all things to work together for good. So even when you miss it, he shows up.

—Bill

Closing Thoughts

Is there an area in your life where you need to surrender to God so that you can know his peace? Is there an area in your life where you need to believe in God's always-good love and get out of the boat?

If you have areas like this where you're finding it hard to trust God, list some of the reasons why. What thoughts are you struggling with?

4

WEEK

Small Group Discussion Questions

These questions will be discussed at your small group meeting.

1. *In your opinion, what should faith look like?*

When have you seen an example of someone living with faith?

2. What does it mean to you for your story to "end well"?

Has there been a time in your life when something bad happened, but God used it for good? Share about that experience.

3. *Jesus went to bat for us regarding the crisis of identity. The moment we ask God to be the King of our journey, we have access to our Christlike identity. How often do you think of yourself as a child of God?*

What does it mean to you to know that you are a child of God?

4. *God's love is the foundation upon which we can leap into obedience even if it looks risky—especially if it looks risky. Is there a risky leap God is inviting you to take regarding business, family, education, or relationship?*

Sometimes extending forgiveness to those who have hurt or disappointed us is the riskiest, most difficult leap to take. Is there someone in your life who has hurt you, and who you have yet to forgive? What do you think might happen if you were to forgive that person?

5. *The peace that surpasses understanding is available to those who give up the right to understand. When we surrender our rights to understand, God gives us his peace. What is an area in your life you could surrender so you might know peace?*

Often we want a miracle, but very rarely are we willing to put ourselves in a situation in which we need one. God is looking for sons and daughters who are willing to "get out of the boat." What is an area in your life where you need to live untamed and trust in him?

6. *What is one step you can take that will bring you closer to obedience, whether it's by forgiveness, reaching out to someone, or taking a leap of faith?*

Are you ready to take that step of faith? If not, what will it take for you to believe?

On Earth as It Is in Heaven

Opening Thoughts

- When you think of the phrase "heaven on earth," what images, emotions, or thoughts come to mind?

- Today and every day this week, while you are going through your routines, pay attention to the people around you and what their needs are. Try to do one thoughtful thing for someone each day that you wouldn't normally do.

- Do you see yourself as a vessel of God's love? Is your life becoming more selfish or more self-less? What legacy do you want to leave the world?

■ Day 1: Love Works

After saying yes to Jesus, we must understand that salvation is not just a moment—it's a continual state of mind. Our salvation is not the end of our story; it's the beginning of a new one. And our task is to bring heaven to earth while we are alive through our words and our actions.

But what does "heaven on earth" mean, exactly? The first thing we have to know in order to model that behavior for earth is to understand what heaven is like. When we look at scripture, we get a good idea of what heaven is like: heaven is beautiful (Revelation 21:2); heaven is full of continuous praise and worship (Isaiah 6:3); and people of all races, languages, and cultures are represented in heaven (Revelation 7:9). This means that every action we take here should have one result in mind—to make our world as beautiful as heaven through a devoted relationship with God and encouraging and loving others, regardless of who they are, what they look like, or where they live.

While it's true that we can just sit back and, being secure in our own salvation, never reach out to others, that's doing a disservice to ourselves, to others, and to God. We are called to do so much more than exist. We're called to live life to the fullest and give life to others.

That might sound a little scary, especially if you're a shy person. Maybe you're not good with words or maybe you feel that your faith is a private matter and you don't want to share your thoughts with others. But how is that love? Why would you want to keep a good thing from someone else?

Romans 12:9 says, "Let love be genuine" (ESV). And in John 13:34–35, Jesus reminds us that to love, we must take action: "A new commandment I give to you, that you love one another: just as I have loved you, you also are to love one another. By this all people will know that you are my disciples, if you have love for one another" (ESV).

You don't have to be a pastor to share the love of God. You don't have to be a good speaker. You don't even have to have Bible verses memorized. If you worry too much about how you're dressed, how you phrase it, or how sincere you sound, you start to lose that necessary quality of being genuine. In fact, all you have to do is begin to incorporate love into everything you do and say. When you speak or act with sincerity, there's a love in action that cannot be hidden, no matter how clumsy you may be.

As we learn to accept and truly appreciate our own salvation, our hearts should become softer. Our view should become wider. Our words should become gentler. We should strive daily to become love in action. As we do this, we get one step closer to bringing heaven to earth. And hopefully, we are able to help other people on their journeys as well.

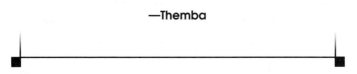

Jesus said when you pray, pray "your kingdom come," and the first place the kingdom of God comes and is evident is in our hearts and lives. My understanding of the Scripture is that when we pray, God first changes us. And as he changes us, we are able to change and transform the environment around us.

—Themba

Closing Thoughts

Is it possible that your new journey is about establishing God's kingdom on earth as it is in heaven? What's that look like for you?

How do you imagine the world or simply your environment could change as a result of God's will being done on earth as it is in heaven?

■ Day 2: "Everything I Have Is Yours"

I love the story of the prodigal son. It has always been one of my favorites because it talks about the amazing unmerited mercy and grace of a good father.

In this famous parable, there was a father with two sons. The younger son came to his father and asked for his inheritance. The father gave it to him and the younger son went out into the world and spent it in every self-centered way conceivable. Eventually he ran out of cash. Then the country went into a recession and the only job he could find was feeding pigs. He hit bottom when he realized that the pigs ate better than he did. So he decided to go home, beg forgiveness, and ask his father for a place among the servants.

When the father saw his son returning home, he rushed out to meet his son and immediately began planning a celebration feast. There was eating, laughing, singing, and dancing late into the night as mercy and grace passed through the room like good wine. But the story doesn't end there. There's an epilogue where we don't want one. It's distracting and, honestly, a little sad and disappointing.

The prodigal son's older brother was in the field when he heard music and dancing in the distance. Surprised, he called one of the servants and asked him what was going on. When he heard that his younger brother had returned and was being celebrated, he "became angry and refused to go in. So his father went out and pleaded with him. But he answered his father, 'Look! All these years I've been slaving for you and never disobeyed your orders. Yet you never gave me even a young goat so I could celebrate with my friends. But when this son of yours who has squandered your property with prostitutes comes home, you kill the fattened calf for him!'" (Luke 15:28–30). (Let's face it, you and I probably would have reacted the same way.) When the son was done ranting at his father for celebrating the disobedient younger brother, the father responded with love and patience, saying, "My son . . . you are always with me, and everything I have is yours" (v. 31).

I ache for the older brother in this story because he was living out of a faith based on religion rather than relationship. When we live outside the context of relationship, we see nothing but rules, and we are unable to celebrate when a beautiful relationship is restored.

I have met many Christians who have been hurt by the goodness of God because they have been living and doing all the right things for all the wrong reasons. Like the older brother, if we don't understand that everything that belongs to our father also belongs to us, we miss out on not only the celebration but also our potential and full strength. We find ourselves toiling away with access to only our own limited abilities and strength, and resenting our heavenly Father. We find ourselves at odds with the very nature that is our Father's love.

However, when we see our inheritance for what it is, the very power of love, we no longer need worry or fret. We need never slave again. We are heirs to the King. Everything he has is ours and it is ours right now. Not because of what we have done but because of what Jesus did. Because we are now heirs, every aspect of our Father is available to us.

*Jesus is alive in me . . . And I believe
that as he lives through me, I allow
him to bring heaven to earth through
my life, through people that I meet
and circumstances that I'm in.*

—Mary

Closing Thoughts

Is it possible that the kingdom of heaven is available to us now? And if so, what kind of impact does this revelation have on your life?

In what ways do you allow Jesus to bring heaven to earth through your life?

■ Day 3: Wide Open Places

"Enter through the narrow gate. For wide is the gate and broad is the road that leads to destruction, and many enter through it. But small is the gate and narrow the road that leads to life, and only a few find it." (Matthew 7:13–14)

I have heard these two verses of Scripture taught from the pulpit many times. And mostly, they have been delivered as a warning. The message would come with a cautionary tale of people who fell off the narrow road into sin. There was always a sense that once we accept Jesus into our hearts, we have a long, narrow, and restricted journey to look forward to. In all honesty, the narrow-road teaching has never sounded like much fun.

What I find interesting is directly before the narrow-road comments, when Jesus talked about God's expansive goodness:

> Ask, and you will receive. Search, and you will find. Knock, and the door will be opened for you. Everyone who asks will receive. Everyone who searches will find. And the door will be opened for everyone who knocks. Would any of you give your hungry child a stone, if the child asked for some bread? Would you give your child a snake if the child asked for a fish? As bad as you are, you still know how to give good gifts to your children. But your heavenly Father is even more ready to give good things to people who ask. Treat others as you want them to treat you. This is what the Law and the Prophets are all about." (vv. 7–12 CEV)

He described how most of humanity isn't aware of how much God wants to give to us, how receiving from God is as simple as asking. He described God as a good and loving Father who wishes to give us our heart's desires—quite a contrast to the bleak way most interpret "narrow-road" Christianity. In doing so, it seems Jesus was providing the proper context for interpretation of the narrow-gate, narrow-road passage, as he laid the groundwork for an incredible truth found in these verses.

Jesus referred to himself as the narrow gate and the narrow road. He knew the plan for his life, and he gave his listeners a foreshadowing of what was to come. He knew he was going to die and rise from the dead, and he knew in doing this he would make life abundantly available to us. That's what he told us in

John 10:10: "I have come that they may have life, and that they may have it more abundantly" (NKJV).

To walk through the small gate and follow the narrow road is a decision to surrender to God and ask him into our hearts. It is this path that leads us to a treasure beyond imagination, a relationship with the King and citizenship in his kingdom. This kingdom is beyond what we can ask for or imagine, but Jesus makes it clear we are still to ask and to imagine.

The kingdom of heaven is the "life" Jesus referred to. The kingdom is not something we enter at our physical death. The kingdom is something we get to live here on earth. So let's get this scripture right. It's not a restrictive works-based religion we've entered into; it's a wide-open love affair. It's simply saying yes to his love and yes to becoming love.

> *Often people will use a justification of the verse, "The poor will always be with you," to say that poverty is OK and that injustice is OK because God is still perfecting us and we're waiting for a better life. I think God wants that better life to be now. God wants and longs for justice for the oppressed now. He longs for the poor to have everything they need now.*
>
> **—Megan**

Closing Thoughts

Would you agree that Jesus is the narrow gate referenced in Matthew 7:13–14, and if so, what does your life look like once you have entered through the gate?

How often do you truly believe that God will meet your needs?

■ Day 4: The Possibilities

Earlier in this study, we talked about the Ten Commandments and how we sometimes try to live our lives from a religious checklist instead of a love relationship. Before Jesus' death and resurrection, followers of God could structure their lives from a set of rules. But as a result of Jesus' death on the cross, God-followers are invited into a relationship with him.

Oftentimes we as believers will try to go back to a checklist rule-based Christianity, especially when we want something that seems like it falls outside of a love relationship with God. The truth is, a relationship costs something. And sometimes it just seems easier to settle for living from a checklist. But in reality, that can actually limit our possibilities for how we relate to God and to others.

The problem is, there is no such thing as a checklist gospel. Since Jesus' death and resurrection, there has been no part of the Christian life, no part of this journey, that was possible without relationship. Not one part of following God is doable outside of a relationship with him.

The New Testament is full of scriptures that sound like impossibilities:

- "Be joyful always" (1 Thessalonians 5:16).

- "Give thanks in all circumstances" (1 Thessalonians 5:18).

- "Be holy, because I am holy" (1 Peter 1:16).

- "Love your enemies" (Matthew 5:44).

Most of us, myself included, tend to think there are definitely some things we need God's help with, but also some things we can do without him. You know, "I need him at church but not at work. I need him at prayer time but not at the grocery store." That sort of thing. And there are parts of the New Testament we don't know what to do with. Like the scriptures I referenced, they just don't seem possible.

As a result, we tend to split life into two categories—sacred and secular—when the truth is that every part of this new journey with Jesus is sacred and holy. None of it is possible without him. On this side of the cross, a journey with Jesus is not segmented into secular or sacred and it is not determined by what we can or can't understand. It's all about knowing and being known by him. And it's this relationship that encompasses every nuance of life— be it at church or work, in prayer or at the grocery store.

We aren't living a checklist gospel; we are living a Good News gospel. Love came down and saved us spiritually, emotionally, and physically. We are saved through surrendering to love. Since the cross, we no longer are called to a religion; we are in a relationship with Jesus that makes all of life sacred and the impossible possible.

I agree that it's a radical thought, the idea that this entire journey is sacred and that the seeming impossibilities of what Jesus calls us to are actually possible. But there is a great opportunity to know God more fully when we are simply willing to read the "impossible" scriptures with openness to possibility.

I am challenged when I read the words of Jesus: "Be holy, because I am holy" or "Give thanks in all circumstances." However, God can reveal his heart to me in these scriptures if I am willing to say, "Even though my experience doesn't line up with this verse, and even though I can't fully understand it, I am going to remain open to the possibility." In essence, I won't allow my lack of understanding to disqualify me from knowing the heart of God behind a certain verse. Instead I will press deeper into a relationship with Jesus that I might know him more fully and so become more like him.

The Christian journey is about a relationship with God in every aspect of life. It's a journey where we begin to see impossibilities become possible.

The love of God is and has to be practical and it has to be demonstrated by me as a human to you as a human and to the people around me . . . or it's pointless.

—Rogan

Closing Thoughts

Is there an "impossibility" in your life today that you can choose to believe God for? What is it? What do you want the outcome to be?

In what ways do you view the love of God as practical?

■ Day 5: The Reformation

The Bible says the kingdom of God is always advancing (Matthew 11:12). There is a reformation always in motion, a revolution always at work. In our faith journey, we are growing, maturing, and changing. We are becoming like Jesus. The moment we said yes to Jesus, we stepped into a continual personal reformation. Here are a couple examples of what that looks like in our lives:

- "We . . . are being transformed into his likeness with ever-increasing glory, which comes from the Lord, who is the Spirit" (2 Corinthians 3:18).

- "For those God foreknew he also predestined to be conformed to the likeness of his Son" (Romans 8:29).

My ten-year-old daughter is currently missing six teeth. Her adult teeth are causing a reformation inside her mouth. Her mouth is being reformed. Now, she did not choose to lose six teeth, and certainly not all at once. It's just what happens; it's called growing.

However, unlike my daughter who has no choice but to accept the coming teeth, we as believers can make decisions to stop growing, to stop changing—to end a personal reformation. The moment we stop believing in the always-good love of God in an area of life, we effectively choose to end the reformation. We can either choose to believe God is good and loving, or not. We can either receive his love or shut down communion with him.

Walking with God is always about growth. If we are not growing in God's love, we have missed the point of the journey. God is continually inviting us to know his love in greater measure in every aspect of life. And saying yes to his love always results in reformation as we are transformed into Jesus' likeness.

All along the journey we are presented with opportunities to either believe or not, to grow or maintain. Regardless, Jesus loves us right now just the way we are, and he loves us right now for who we will become. God's kingdom is always advancing "on earth as it is in heaven." We have been invited to play a role in its advancement. The moment we ask Jesus to be our friend and Savior, we enter into a relationship with him and the journey begins. This Christian journey is about reformation; it's about a transformed mind and a new heart. It's about receiving the love of God and

establishing his kingdom of love in the here and now. It's about being transformed into his likeness so we can see like Jesus, hear like Jesus, walk and talk and love like Jesus. May God bless you on the journey! It's truly worth everything you have, everything you are, and everything you hope to become.

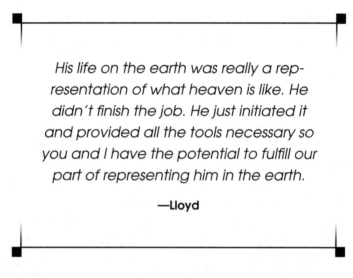

His life on the earth was really a representation of what heaven is like. He didn't finish the job. He just initiated it and provided all the tools necessary so you and I have the potential to fulfill our part of representing him in the earth.

—Lloyd

Closing Thoughts

In what area of your life is the reformation of heaven on earth taking place?

How often do you think of yourself as representing Christ here on earth?

Small Group Discussion Questions

These questions will be discussed at your small group meeting.

1. *What are the first things that come to mind when you hear the phrase "on earth as it is in heaven"?*

Has anyone ever shared the love of God with you? What happened? What was that experience like?

2. *God's kingdom is available to us because of Jesus' death and resurrection. In what way can you intentionally establish God's kingdom of love in your life and in the lives of those around you?*

3. *As sons and daughters of God, everything he has is ours. We have been given access to his entire heavenly kingdom. What are some of the attributes of heaven that you want to see established in your life, such as wholeness, healing, restoration, peace, and joy?*

How do you envision the attribute(s) you mentioned changing your life or the lives of people around you?

4. Jesus is the gate through which we enter his wide-open love journey. In what areas of life have you been living without freedom to dream?

5. We serve a God who makes the impossible possible. When have you experienced something that you thought was impossible become possible?

How can you become intentional about pursuing God past that which appears impossible?

6. *If you knew you could not fail, what would you attempt to do in this life? No matter how far-fetched your dreams may seem, they are possible. Think of several steps you can take to move closer to those dreams.*

The Open Table Series with Donald Miller

The Open Table DVD, Volume 1
978-1-4185-1099-2, $29.99

The Open Table Participant's Guide, Volume 1
978-1-4185-1095-4, $9.99

The Open Table: An Invitation to Know God is simply that—an open invitation for discussion about some of life's greatest questions: what is Christianity, who is Jesus, and how should this affect our lives? Donald Miller invites you to join him in a conversation infused with humor, truth, history, and above all, honesty. Whether you have never opened a Bible or if you grew up reciting the Lord's Prayer, the table is open to you.

The Open Table DVD, Volume 2
978-1-4185-1093-0, $29.99

The Open Table Participant's Guide, Volume 2
978-1-4185-1089-3, $9.99

The first volume of The Open Table series explored the person and deity of Christ. Now discover what it means to not only know him but walk with him. *The Open Table: An Invitation to Walk with God* is a guide to cultivating and nurturing your soul in such a way that something can grow, something that will sustain you—namely, a relationship with God.

Join the conversation: www.JoinTheOpenTable.com.

Jazz Notes is the literary equivalent of a remix CD

NONRELIGIOUS THOUGHTS ON CHRISTIAN SPIRITUALITY

DONALD MILLER

JAZZ NOTES

Improvisations on
BLUE LIKE JAZZ

Cool sound-bytes strategically crafted from Don Miller's classic *Blue Like Jazz*, combined with brand-new material that offers the author's fans an inside look at some of the unforgettable—and outrageous—characters and stories from the original best seller.

Jazz Notes includes a bonus audio CD with Don Miller interview.

The Journey of a Million Miles Begins with a Single Step . . . Buying the Book.

A Million Miles in a Thousand Years
from *New York Times* best-selling author
Donald Miller

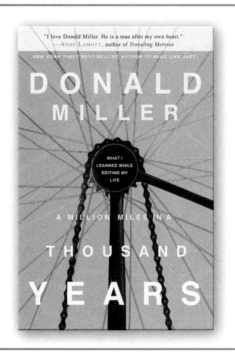

Full of beautiful, heart-wrenching, and hilarious stories, *A Million Miles in a Thousand Years* details one man's opportunity to edit his life as if he were a character in a movie.

Join the conversation:
facebook.com/donaldmillerfan, twitter.com/donmilleris